Ma Ganga

and the Razai Box

Geeta Dharmarajan

Art by Sonali Biswas

KATHA

When Yasho looked out of her window, it was raining. Pouring!

She looked at the mountains, dark and heavy. And there was Ganga jumping and tripping over the rocks, carrying the mud formed over the ages into the sea.

"Another flood!" Yasho thought. Doesn't Ma Ganga know that our trees can't grow without the soil she carries off.

Yasho stomped to the river. "Ganga!" she called out boldly. "How dare you take our soil to the sea?"

"How dare you speak to me like that, Young Yasho of the Hill People!" It was almost as if Ma Ganga's voice spoke from inside Yasho.

"I don't want your soil. Do you think I want to look all muddy? And don't I know the top few inches of soil are important for the village? But if you don't care about it, why should I? Once long ago, Shiva spread his matted hair before me. Find me Shiva's hair and I won't flood your homes. Till then, I'm going my way!"

And, spying Yasho's razai box in a corner, Ma Ganga jumped into it!

Soon, the whole village got to know that Ma Ganga was in Yasho's razai box. The Panchayat was furious. "How dare you trap Ma Ganga," they scolded Yasho. "Quick, let her out."

But when they went to fetch her, Ma Ganga was fast asleep inside Yasho's razai box.

Awakened by their pleas, she said sleepily, "I'll give you a year. And if in a year's time you have not found me Shiva's locks, I don't want to come back to your village. I'm tired of always taking the blame." So saying, she turned on her side.

"Ma," said Yasho, putting her head close to the box, "give us a little time. I promise you'll have your wish."

The puzzled villagers gathered under the peepal tree to find a way out. “Shiva’s matted locks? What did Ganga mean by that?” said one. “What could she mean by that?” chorused all the villagers.

“Friends,” said Yasho, “I think we can give Ma Ganga what she wants.”

"But how?" cried the Hill People.

"There's a way," said Yasho, her voice bubbling with joy. "Let's plant trees everywhere. The roots and branches of trees are like Shiva's hair. They will hold the soil. They'll make Ma Ganga happy!"

The people looked at their barren hills and their muddy stream.

It would need a lot of work. Still, a small wise voice inside each of them said that Yasho

was right. There was a time when their hills were green and bountiful. Yasho's idea could turn their village green again!

The people worked as never before. It was as if the whole village was alive again. Somehow they had to find – "or make," said Yasho – Shiva's matted locks. Otherwise, they would have to go without water.

A year went by. Ganga came out to see how the Hill People were doing. "Good!" she thought to herself, as she played with the kids and rumbled over her old bed. "The people are seeing sense once more!"

"Please stay with us," the Hill People begged.

"You still have some work left," said Ma Ganga. And back she climbed into Yasho's razai box.

In the wink of an eye, two years were gone. Yasho and the villagers went to coax Ma Ganga out of the razai box.

And what did she see? There once again were trees and shrubs springing all over the hills and valleys.

"Ah! Their roots are like Shiva's matted hair," said Ma Ganga. The sun that shone down smiled in each one of her countless dimples.

"Thank you! I'm happy to be back with you!" Ma Ganga said, as she once again giggled and gurgled her way to the sea, clear as clear can be!

reduced all of the sixty thousand princes to ashes.

For years King Sagar's descendents offered penance and prayer to set their souls free. But Sage Kapil was unmoved, and the ghosts of Sagar's sons wandered restlessly for seven generations.

Until Bhagiratha vowed to bring Ganga down to earth, so she could carry his ancestors' ashes back to heaven.

Bhagiratha prayed and performed rituals so strict that Lord Brahma agreed to send Ganga down to earth. She could not disobey the Creator's command. So she leapt from the heavens, determined to sweep the earth away with the force of her waters. But Bhagiratha beseeched Shiva to break her fall.

Lord Shiva undid his matted locks. As she hurtled downwards, with one great sweep of his head, he spread them across the sky. There, he caught her and released her slowly, bidding her to always follow Bhagiratha in her descent from the icy cave.

Touched by the three Gods, she became the holiest of rivers on earth. The sixty thousand souls of King Sagar's sons attained salvation. And ever since, people have come to Ma Ganga to purify their lives.

THE STORY OF GANGA

It is believed that Ganga Devi
was born from Brahma's water pot, his kamandalu, when he washed the feet of Vishnu in his Vamana incarnation. She is the daughter of the mighty Meru, whom we call Himalaya. Her sister is Uma, Shiva's companion. For an eternity she danced and sparkled in the heavens, delighting Indra and the gods.

Then King Sagar performed the Ashwamedh Yagya for his kingdom. He sent his horse to roam the land, annexing all the territories it crossed. Indra, fearing that Sagar would grow more powerful than he, stole the horse and hid it close to where the sage Kapil sat in deep meditation.

Now King Sagar had sixty thousand sons. He sent them off in search of the horse. They stormed Kapil's ashram, shouting and cursing. The sage woke from his trance, eyes blazing and with one wrathful glance,

SOIL EROSION

The Ganga is one of the world's greatest rivers. It is India's longest river, flowing over 2,500 km, down the Himalaya mountains, and across the plains to the Bay of Bengal. Like all great rivers, the Ganga is important to both human and animal life. Over 400 million people live in villages, towns and cities by the Ganga. The forests and grasslands, the shores and waters along the river are home to many different animals, birds, reptiles and fish.

To all Hindus, the Ganga is the most sacred of rivers. She is Ma Ganga, a living mother goddess and the symbol of purity. It is sad that the Ganga is also one of the most polluted rivers in the world. Sewage, chemicals and rubbish are dumped into the river every day. This means that people who rely on the river for their needs often become sick from drinking the water. Pollution also puts many rare and amazing creatures, like the Ganges river dolphin into the danger of disappearing altogether.

Another big problem is soil erosion. It is natural for rivers to carry away some soil with them. However, when the soil is left exposed because too many trees are cut down, or due to over-grazing, cultivation, or fire, it happens much faster than normal. The rich layer of top soil is swept away by the water. Once this is gone, few plants will grow in the soil again. Without soil and plants, the land becomes unable to support life. This process is called desertification. It is very difficult and often impossible to restore desertified land. To replace an inch of washed away topsoil, plants and other matter on the surface must break down for hundreds or even thousands of years. Erosion can damage roads and bridges. It can cause pollution of waterways and flash floods, when it occurs rapidly. Replacing the soil nutrients carried out to sea by our rivers each year with fertilizer would cost crores of rupees.

Plants protect the soil and prevent erosion. They slow down water as it flows over the land. Roots hold the soil in position so it cannot be washed away. Plants break the force of a raindrop before it hits the soil, so most of the rain can soak into the ground. Plants along river banks are especially important, as they slow down the flow of the water and their roots bind the soil. Allowing natural plants to grow along the river banks instead of planting crops right up to the water's edge and planting several different types of plants together, are other good ways of preventing erosion.

Geeta Dharmarajan founded Katha in 1988, with a children's magazine called *Tamasha!*. Her deep interest in social work in education led to the development of a special story-based pedagogy and curriculum for children coming from underserved communities. She views stories as a means of fostering unity by reinforcing diversity. Previously, she was one of the editors of *The Pennsylvania Gazette*, the magazine of the Ivy League University of Pennsylvania, and *Target*, a magazine for children which marked the beginning of her 31 years of professional editorial experience. She has 31 books and over 400 published pieces to her credit.

Sonali Biswas is a freelance illustrator based in Delhi. She is the recipient of The Chitra Katha Award 2003 for Outstanding Illustrations for *One Lonely Unicorn*, a story-counting book published by Katha. She has also received the Runner-Up award from Noma Concours for Children's Book Illustrations in 2000 and an Honourable Mention at the Biennial of Asian Illustrators, Japan in 2002.

KATHA

First published © Katha, 2006

Printed in New Delhi

ISBN 978-81-89020-74-3

Our Mission: Every child reading well for fun and meaning!
KATHA is a registered nonprofit organization started in 1988. Devoted to enhancing the joys of reading amongst children and adults, we work with more than 1,00,000 children in poverty, to bring them to grade-level reading through quality books and interventions.

Delhi: A225, Shivalik, Malviya Nagar, New Delhi 110 017
Chennai: 21-G, ARK Colony, Eldams Rd, Chennai, Tamil Nadu 600018
Phone: Delhi: +91 11 4182 9998 | Chennai: +91 98400 30073
Email: books@katha.org
Websites: www.katha.org | books.katha.org | 300m.katha.org

The profits from this book will support the quality education of children studying in Katha schools.
Katha regularly plants trees to replace the wood used in the making of its books.

First Reprint 2012, Second Reprint 2015, Third Reprint 2016, Fourth Reprint 2017, Fifth Reprint 2023, Sixth Reprint 2025
Seventh Reprint 2025